Pre-Colonial

AFRICAN SLAVERY:
A History of Fake Facts

Trevor

M.

Millett

PREFACE

Using a radical historian as a sounding board for this essay, *Pre-Colonial African Slavery: A History of Fake Facts,* I was advised that it would not receive a warm welcome in conventional scholarly circles. The historian, though radical and a supporter of Black Power, subscribes to the orthodoxy of slavery being an ancient institution in sub-Saharan Africa. He felt the essay would find no supporters among respected historians. But I would have none of it. His warning fell on deaf ears. I had high hopes.

Sending the essay to a reputable English journal with international standing in the world of academia—a journal that serves as a platform for discussions about slavery and abolition—I assumed the essay would easily pass muster and provoke reflection on the need for authentic primary research to be done on the subject. I would be sorely disappointed. After waiting some time, I got their response.

Once the board members of the journal had read the essay, their response was addressed to "Dr Millett." I never said I was a PhD. I never even hinted at such a thing. I presented myself truthfully as a mere commoner. But after reading the essay, the professorial board (all of them well-known historians internationally) bestowed an honorary doctorate on me, which suggests they thought the essay had merit, but it was far too controversial and subversive to be touched by them. And they suggested that I do more research on the matter before making my claim.

In other words, the very sources of misinformation that I was challenging were to be used for extensive research to strengthen and invigorate my argument against the fallacious claim that slavery in sub-Saharan Africa was of ancient pedigree. The accused would be his own judge, prosecutor, and jury. The whole point of the essay is to challenge the legitimacy of that baseless claim and to question the works of historians which rest on that dubious claim.

Therefore, the recommendation of the journal's board was, in my mind, tantamount to me being advised to conscript enemy forces to fight my battle for me. That way, victory would never come. The narrative would remain unchanged. I found it highly ironical that the journal would make that recommendation. Then again, their stance shouldn't be surprising because they are stakeholders in that fictitious world which I feel is in urgent need of redress. I continue to feel strongly about the matter. Very much so.

Realizing I was on a fool's errand trying to win support from established academicians, whose reputations and careers probably would have been built on the false claim of slavery in sub-Saharan Africa being a reality seemingly from time immemorial, I thought it best to publish the essay independently.

Hopefully, as a thinking, dispassionate, impartial reader, having no stake in maintaining a scholarly fiction, you will find merit in the arguments presented here. I sincerely hope you do.

AFRICAN SLAVERY: MYTH OR REALITY?

Of the origins of slavery in ancient pre-colonial sub-Saharan Africa, we know very little; indeed, basically nothing. There has been no in-depth original or primary research to excavate the truth and prove that slavery actually existed in Africa south of the Sahara dating back to antiquity, independent of and prior to Arab and European intrusions. How, when, and exactly why would the institution have emerged in sub-Saharan Africa are mysteries left largely unsolved by historians because there is absolutely no conclusive research about the pre-colonial inception of slavery in those parts of the continent. We know nothing of the principal or key factors that would have necessitated the establishment of an indigenous institution of slavery, generally perceived as coterminous with its westernized counterpart, in territories of sub-Saharan Africa. What would have been the justifiable triggers for such an institution? All we have are rebellious questions unquelled by irrefutable authoritative answers.

HISTORY GROUNDED IN GUESSWORK

To appease and seduce us into accepting the supposed truism of slavery in sub-Saharan Africa, we are offered this commonly made statement: "Systems of servitude and slavery were common in parts of Africa in ancient times, as they were in much of the rest of the ancient world."

That, from *Wikipedia* which is today's global encyclopedia for information and enlightenment. But that is fabricated information which has assumed the status of fact due to a prolonged process of "refinement" and legitimization based on interminable monotonous repetition. Because sub-Saharan Africa formed part of the ancient world, the confident claim for slavery existing and being practised in those parts has never struck us as suspect. Confirmation bias has disposed us to believe the worst about sub-Saharan Africans. Moreover, given the routine historical portraiture and stereotypical depiction of Africans as a naturally servile people, the claim, when made, has never warranted seemingly unnecessary questions about its legitimacy and accuracy.

In effect, prejudice has written the history of ancient or prehistoric sub-Saharan Africa. Those with biases who initially assumed the responsibility to write that history created the "facts" to suit their preconceived notions about sub-Saharan African civilization. Since in their minds and according to the colourful conventions of their times, Africans were supposed to be naturally servile and subservient, then their "facts" were tailored to substantiate and match those opinions, suspicions, beliefs and expectations. They carried within their souls the firm belief in a sub-human species that was uninteresting, uninventive, and stagnant. They were the creators of an exotic Africa that did not exist in history.

Thus, the claim for slavery in ancient sub-Saharan Africa does not rest on a foundation of solid authentic facts or on detailed reliable documents. The claim shows no respect for any known standard of proof. It does not satisfy that factual burden in any convincing way. As the writer Thomas C. Foster has rightfully observed, "Facts are facts. They are objectively verifiable without manipulation. This is not to say they are not contentious, which is part of what makes life interesting. But only fools and knaves deny facts themselves" (*2022, p. 233*).[1/] Or, acting irresponsibly, they dare to make bold claims unsupported by facts or documents.

The editor of UNESCO's *General History of Africa II - - Ancient Civilizations of Africa* (which covers the period 7000 B.C. to 700 A.D.), G. Mokhtar, has actually confessed in the Introduction to the volume that much of what passes for the history of that period is based largely on "supposition." But informed conjecture, reasonable speculation or educated guesses cannot and should not be embraced as solid authentic facts. They are controvertible hypotheses. They are the starting point for serious research, not its conclusive end. However, Prof. Mokhtar strongly suggests we should be accommodating and accepting of such:

> This volume of *A General History of Africa*, perhaps even more than the volume that preceded it, must depend on suppositions. The period it covers is

obscure, owing to the scarcity of sources in general, and of solidly dated sources in particular. This applies both to the very uneven collections of archaeological sources and to the written or pictorial sources, except in respect of certain relatively privileged regions such as the Nile valley and the Maghrib. It is this lack of documentary bases that makes it necessary to resort to suppositions, since facts established with certainty are always the exception.

Another point should be stressed: the archaeological sources available to the historian are extremely inadequate. Excavations are not uniformly spread over the continent as a whole. There is not everywhere the density of excavations that is found notably along the coast, in the hinterland of the northern fringe and, above all, in the Nile valley from the sea to the Second Cataract.

This lack of archaeological information cannot, unfortunately, be supplemented by the reports of foreign travellers, contemporaries of the events or facts that concern this volume. The continent's rugged nature, and its very size, discouraged, in antiquity as later, deep penetration by those from the outside....

These considerations explain why the history of Africa, from -7000 to +700, still consists largely of suppositions. However, these suppositions are never unfounded; they are based on information, rare and inadequate certainly, but which exists none the less (*1981, p.2*).[2]

Herodotus, the Father of History, (ca. 484-425 BC)[3/] and Ibn Battuta, the 14th century Muslim Moroccan scholar and explorer, mostly express their fierce anti-black biases in their writings about Africa. They do not actually address how, why, and when slavery was instituted in sub-Saharan Africa. They do not provide us with information about the compelling ancient triggers that initially engendered slavery in sub-Saharan Africa. Herodotus furnishes us with unflattering descriptions of Africans. Battuta, however, does talk explicitly about Africans being naturally "submissive to slavery," about slave raids being carried out in East Africa, and of the Sudanese as a people who "steal each other's children and sell them to merchants." The 10th century geography book, "Boundaries of the World" (*Hudud al-Alam*), written by an unknown Persian, also makes mention of "slaves and servants" in West Africa, but little else.

PROOF-LESS SHODDY SCHOLARSHIP

In discussing the issue of slavery in sub-Saharan Africa, historians, such as Leslie B. Rout, Philip D. Curtin, Roger Anstey, W.E.B. Du Bois, Eric Williams, J.E. Inikori, Walter Rodney, among many others, are all engaged statistically and developmentally with the population losses suffered by African communities impacted by slave raiders and kidnappers and the huge profits derived from the various slave "trades" which helped to develop Europe and fuel the Industrial Revolution in Britain and other parts of Europe. Orlando Patterson, John W. Blassingame et al focus on the sociological and cultural aspects of slavery in discussing the subject.

Nobody delves deeply into the origins of slavery as a particular subject of interest, in and of itself, and as an essential foundational feature of sub-Saharan African civilization. It is generally taken for granted that slavery did exist there. For the most part, the discourse begins with an unproven claim about the antiquity of slavery in Africa, then, using circular logic, the narrative spirals from this pseudo-scholastic soil into a giant sequoia bearing the poisonous fruit of historical deception. The critical scholarly imperative to prove and establish that slavery was an immemorial fact of life in sub-Saharan Africa, as the prerequisite and necessary prologue to a valid discussion of the subject matter, is disregarded altogether. The proof, it seems, resides in the claim, per se, which feeds self-sustainingly upon itself for validity. This, to say the least, is scandalously shoddy scholarship.

The discourse about African slavery revolves mostly around the trans-Atlantic slave "trade," covering the period from the 15th to the 19th century, as the starting point and the meat of the whole subject matter. Mention is sometimes made of the Islamic, trans-Saharan "trade" which originated in the 7th century and very infrequently the Indian Ocean or East African slave "trade." It is estimated that between 7-10 million lives were caught up in the slave "trade" across the Sahara. That estimate includes those who died on the desert's edge and those lost on the journey across the desert. Overall, the size of the human traffic to the entire Muslim world is estimated at 11-17 million individuals.

Even at this point, however, we find ourselves ensnared using the term "trade." Who decided that each of these unsavoury illegal trafficking activities in men, women and children should be characterized, defined, legitimized, and dignified in this way? Africans? Did they regard themselves as "commodities"? Basically, everything about slavery and the slave "trade" linked to sub-Saharan Africa is mediated and filtered by western (less so Arabic) perspectives, prejudices, principles, and preferences. Slavery is discussed as a topic largely within western history. Arab scholars have their own reasons for avoiding the subject.

In addressing this vexing problem, we take note of Walter Rodney's observation about the imbalance of power in the context of academic learning. He argued that the books, the references or citations, the theoretical assumptions, the definitions, and the entire ideological underpinnings of what students must learn in every single discipline generally commend Europe and America as centres of authority and as scholastic ideals to which others should aspire. In effect, based on Rodney's observation, students are taught curricula grounded in "westernization" as normative and universal. It is quite clear that almost all academic discussions, even those pertaining specifically to African realities, are conducted within a distinctly western intellectual and ideological framework, using western terms, concepts, insights, and ideals as the legitimate tools of analysis. Up until the late 1960s, many black intellectuals would not accept "academic truth" unless it was endorsed and validated by the West. Clearly, the colonized personality (hollowed out culturally) has no sense of the legitimacy of its own interests, whatever those interests may be, academic or otherwise.

Social psychologist and activist Dr Amos Wilson makes an even more aggressive statement on this social/political/intellectual power-relations dynamic:

> Every discipline that is practiced in the dominant-group community is dedicated to maintaining the power of that group and the subordination of the subjected group. It is a great deception we face as blacks, when we go into these schools, that the disciplines—psychology, sociology, economics, physics, chemistry, science and so forth—are neutral, value-free and nonpolitical. That is a very, very great deception. To make courses and disciplines appear to be nonpolitical is one of the greatest political strokes of genius ever.

Every institution and discipline, ultimately, are a part of the process of maintaining power relations. That includes not only what is taught in the colleges and universities, but also the institutions that maintain the functioning of society. These institutions, in addition to the family institution, include legal, education[al] and economic institutions, all combining to maintain European dominance (*Wilson, 2019, pp. 101-102*).[4]

VALUE OF GRIOT HISTORIANS IGNORED

Alternatively, as a safeguard, we are compelled to ask questions because there are obvious problems here with the notion that slavery in sub-Saharan Africa preceded the intrusions of Arabs and Europeans. We are compelled to ask, for instance, were there independent reliable African sources of information, uninfluenced by interpreting Arab or Western historians and social scientists, who, on their own, would have acknowledged the existence of slavery in ancient pre-colonial sub-Saharan Africa as a traditional institution? Did griots, the custodians of history in sub-Saharan Africa, often demeaned by Westerners as garblers who lacked intellectual sophistication, ever make such disclosures in their oral historical accounts about an indigenous transnational institution of slavery on the continent? Do we learn from the griots about the earliest roots or the origins of slavery in sub-Saharan Africa?

The sneering contempt displayed by Western historians towards their griot counterparts served to discredit the factual accuracy and reliability of the latter's testimony. But those who have carefully assessed the griots place much store by their oratorical history. Chancellor Williams, among many others, played his part to restore faith in the griots and dignify their work, now acceptable in the modern world as legitimate oral history, despite the persistent attitude of some stubborn Westerners. Williams observed:

> That for which no written record can be found, it was suggested, should not be accepted as history; yet there were still others, though scattered hither and yon over the continent, [who] did not accept this one-sided version of truth; for they had their own cherished record that was transmitted from generation to generation by their oral historians. These were specially trained to receive, remember, and pass on the lore of their tribe in story and song. And they knew how to separate the truth from tall tales and other embellishments that were intended to enhance interest, startle, or entertain.

> In West Africa, important history has to be separated from mere story-telling at the outset, for the elders, who also know the unwritten history, zealously watch for the slightest error on the part of the story-teller (*Williams, 2004, p. 69*).[5]

Since we were encouraged to distrust the griots, then how do we go about judging slavery in Africa on its own merits, using internally generated criteria, values, standards, principles, and ideals, instead of an imposed framework of analysis? And having discovered the true origins, would "slavery" remain a valid, accurate, insightful term to describe and analyze the unearthed African phenomenon? Would scholars remain comfortable and confident in making that bold assertion?

Yet this claim is made with no substantial supporting evidence, except the strength and authoritative nature of the claim itself that slavery was endemic and widespread in sub-Saharan Africa. That claim has become conventional wisdom and is now made as an unassailable fact. It has credibility and plausibility because of the long-sustained conditioning of the world by media practitioners, social scientists, and historians to connect slavery to Africans/black people. Indeed, once the word "slave" is uttered, the picture of a chained, brutalized African or of a coffle of dark-skinned, woolly-headed individuals trekking through Africa's interior to a coastal depot immediately and automatically comes to mind.

Amos Wilson notes: "Through the rewriting of history and restructuring of perspectives, servitude and slavery have been attached to black people, … and people read into the word[s] 'servant' and 'slave,' *black and African*" (*2020, p. 107*).[6] The result of the rewriting of history to give pre-eminence to black people when slavery is being discussed is that Africans, despite the practice of slavery in the Greek and Roman empires as elsewhere, are the ones conceived historically and currently as the world's slaves. Slavery is almost always presented to the world as a distinctly African phenomenon; an institution that is deeply embedded in sub-Saharan African civilization. In short, it is a culturally organic reality. But how true is this claim, especially when provable distinctions, wide in nature, can be made between the westernized slavery of the Americas and the so-called practice of bondage in sub-Saharan Africa?

The impression is given that Africans had a long-established distasteful habit of selling one another as slaves, with the strong preying on the weak to create and maintain the institution. Africans are blamed for selling their "brothers and sisters" into slavery and therefore being significantly responsible for the debacle. In essence, slavery is viewed and treated as a self-inflicted wound by Africans who needed little or no encouragement by Westerners to engage in the practice. Nor did they need encouragement by Arabs, the precursors to European enslavers, for that matter. That has been the long-standing narrative about African slavery. Having said that, questions arise.

EUROPEAN HISTORIANS HAVE THEIR SAY

Is it not particularly curious that it is only in the context of Arab and European catalysts that we speak of slavery in, and the slave "trade" out of, Africa? Why is the context for African slavery never wholly and independently African? We are advised by Paul E. Lovejoy that "Africa was relatively isolated in ancient and medieval times. Before the middle of the fifteenth century, virtually the only contact was along the East African coast, across the Red Sea, and via the Sahara Desert. Those places bordering these frontiers were different from more isolated regions further inland" (*Lovejoy: Africa and Slavery, 2012* (online source))[7]. Those areas identified by Lovejoy figure prominently in the Indian Ocean or East African and trans-Saharan slave "trades" and from the fifteenth century onwards.

With European penetration, we talk of regions inland becoming involved in the trans-Atlantic slave "trade." According to Lovejoy's research, interior trading of "probable antiquity" consisted principally of gold, kola nuts, copper, and salt. He makes no mention of enslaved individuals. It is not difficult to discern a pattern for the genesis and development of the so-called slave "trades" based on existing knowledge. The decision-making process for the initiation and development of slavery in Africa seems always to be located outside the control of sub-Saharan African power. Shouldn't that fact speak to our skeptical or complacent minds? Did Africans, acting independently, conceptualize and institute systems of slavery in their own communities long before the intrusions of Arabs and Europeans? If they did, what would have incentivized these subsistence communities to do so?

WHYS AND WHEREFORES FOR AFRICAN SLAVERY

Anthropologist, writer, and photojournalist John Reader offers us a cursory explanation that appears, at first glance, to have some merit. He identifies as incentives several possible problems that could have led to a system of coercive labour being established in sub-Saharan Africa. To be convincing, however, he comes close to exaggerating the impact of those problems on the lives of sub-Saharan Africans. Reader informs us that survival in most village societies depended on successful husbandry, essentially subsistence agriculture, made particularly "arduous" because of insubstantial rainfall which resulted in soils being impoverished and hardened.

There were also perennial weeds and defiant stout shrubs that had to be dislodged from land under cultivation. Reader notes: "Weeds are a curse…. In recorded instances, African farmers devote up to 54 per cent of their total labour input to the tiresome business of weeding" (*1989, pp. 252-253*)[8]. Technology, such as the wheel and plough, was also absent from the subsistence agriculture of African farmers. "Many African soils are difficult to plough and domesticated draught animals would be susceptible to endemic disease; a more pressing reason was that feeding the animals would place unsustainable demands upon the food-production system" (*p. 254*)[9]; Reader making that claim as if bonded human beings wouldn't do the same.

He goes on. There was also an "elephant problem," with farmers occupying and working the same fertile areas that elephants found most desirable—areas with crops of grain or roots ready for harvest. Reader writes:

> Elephants dominated the African landscape throughout the evolutionary history of humanity. Cohabitation verging on shared destiny has given the elephant a position of respect—even reverence—in people's minds…. For centuries, much of Africa's potential farmland was a continuously changing patchwork of mutually exclusive human and elephant occupation zones, with the elephant limiting opportunities for agricultural expansion and thus restraining the growth of the human population (*pp. 258-259*).[10]

Because of this myriad of problems African farmers needed help, which, according to Reader, took the form of enslaved individuals so that they could succeed at what they were doing. And here Reader steps into the quicksand of contradiction. He begins by informing us that in prehistory people lived exclusively from hunting and gathering but by AD 1500, 99 per cent of the world's population, including the millions residing in sub-Saharan Africa, were sustained by agriculture. In a later chapter (28) he declares, "Few [*sub-Saharan African subsistence*] communities had sufficient labour to satisfy their needs. Life was arduous and unpredictable. Slavery was commonplace" (*p. 289*).[11] He then refers to a study which claims that "between 30 and 60 per cent of the entire [*sub-Saharan African*] population were slaves during historical times" (*p. 291*).[12] Yet in an earlier chapter (25) he reveals, "Subsistence farming in Africa often demands more labour than can be fed with the food that farmers produce" (*p. 249*).[13] Reader also mentions that while "The labour requirements of subsistence agriculture were high; population growth rates were low" and that "agricultural communities in sub-Saharan Africa were barely large enough to feed themselves" (*p. 291*).[14] Reader's total truth is highly contorted.

So, then, were the slaves a starving community wherever they were found in sub-Saharan Africa? And why would inadequately fed farmers, given the meagre production of the difficult soils they were working, acquire more mouths to feed if they were already struggling to produce enough to feed themselves and their families? And where exactly were all the slaves coming from, given the low population growth rates in these sparsely populated communities that could barely look after themselves? Reader readily admits that "Communities in sub-Saharan Africa were always small and dispersed" (*p. 367*),[15] which insinuates that the vast populations of slaves were nowhere present in those communities. Consequently, should we conclude that the generation of slaves was the direct result of pernicious unrelenting social engineering by outside sources? Walter Rodney suggests exactly that.

FOREIGN TRIGGERS FOR AFRICAN SLAVERY

Until Europeans started man-hunting in West Africa and commercializing sinewy black bodies, bondage in sub-Saharan Africa was hardly a phenomenon that attracted attention as an existing extraordinary form of oppression. Nor did it arouse alarm or trepidation as a humanitarian crisis. But it did become a human tragedy of major proportions once Europeans inserted themselves in West African societies and sought to exploit distinctive forms of human interactions and relationships that had no social equivalents in Europe, about which more will be said as we proceed. In effect, Europeans are the ones largely responsible for the problem of slavery in sub-Saharan Africa and then hundreds of years later, after the problem had become deeply rooted in the region, taking action, with much self-congratulation, to "solve" the problem they had created in the first place. In a small publication entitled *West Africa and the Atlantic Slave Trade*, published by the Historical Association of Tanzania, Walter Rodney points out:

> This was a very strange occurrence. The Europeans thought that they were bringing progress to Africa by putting an end to something backward. They thought that there had always been lots of slaves in Africa, and that many people who were sold to the Europeans were already slaves in Africa. In fact the opposite was true, because it was the Europeans who went to Africa to buy slaves, and helped to start and to increase local slavery (*1967, p. 18*).[16]

Prior to exposing the fraudulent European claim that they were the ones who acted to end slavery in sub-Saharan Africa, Rodney made it abundantly clear that:

> Europeans went to the Gambia, Sierra Leone, the Gold Coast and Nigeria and came away saying that three-quarters of the African population were slaves. Three hundred years before, Europeans had noticed some West African kings with numbers of *servants* [*emphasis added*] who were not entirely free, while a few persons actually belonged to a master and worked as agricultural serfs. But that was all—there was no large slave class, such as could be found in West Africa at the end of the Atlantic slave-trade (*p. 17*).[17]

In another 1967 booklet put out by the Historical Association of Tanzania, historian E. A. Alpers takes up the subject of slavery in East Africa. The booklet is entitled *The East African Slave Trade*. He wastes no time in making the claim that the major works on the subject at that time, pioneering studies by Sir Reginald Coupland—*East Africa and Its Invaders (1938)* and *The Exploration of East Africa, 1856-1890 (1939)*—were "not at all satisfactory" (*p. 3*).[18] And why should that be? Because Sir Reginald's "interpretation of the genesis and nature of the East African slave trade clearly reveals his bias and does not stand up under close examination" (*Ibid*).[19] Interestingly enough, Alpers does not challenge Coupland's unproven assertion that slavery was "a common institution among all Africans" for "ages" prior to Arabic intrusion into the interior to conduct trade with indigenous Africans (*p. 4*).[20] This is Alpers' generous concession to Coupland: "No historian of Africa will dispute the assertion that slaves have been exported from East Africa for as long as Coupland has stated" (*Ibid*).[21] "Why wouldn't they?" is a serious question that Alpers fails to ask and therefore leaves entirely unanswered. Why should historians so easily accept and be comfortable with that claim as fact, without substantial supporting evidence?

Coupland was writing in an era under the aegis of an almost hallowed tradition which allowed anyone to safely throw caution to the wind, make specious, if not ridiculous, claims about Africans ("they were coarse, simple-minded, uncreative, infantile people"; "they had no civilization"; "they had invented nothing"; "their village societies displayed arrested development"; "they had no history") knowing there would be no accountability for such claims. People of African Origin are not and have never been the world's beloved people and are often used as scapegoats by others. The world was prepared to believe the worst about Africans; it still does, resulting in a distorted dishonest Eurocentric-structured past serving and sustaining an equally distorted dishonest Eurocentric-structured present. This aspect of Alpers' analysis is therefore quite unsettling because of the blatant contradiction involved.

Obviously Alpers too is a victim of pro-black slavery historical indoctrination. His thinking in this regard is tainted, because he proffers no evidence to support his and Coupland's common claim that African societies had enslaved people "for ages." Taking such a liberty with the facts must be rooted in the casual disregard many social scientists and historians, particularly Western, have had for the whole truth about Africans: Just say anything about Africans and it will be accepted. Say they were slaves from ancient times. Who would dare or bother to challenge that unverified declaration? But in subsequent sections of the work Alpers provides some redeeming criticisms which shows ambivalence on his part because he is not entirely comfortable with the Coupland claims.

Alpers overturns the most important categorical claims by Coupland by pointing out the absence of reliable historical evidence to support them.

It is very clear that the East Africa slave trade as a factor of continuing historical significance traces its roots back no further than the first half of the eighteenth century. Coupland's argument that it was of continuing importance from the earliest contacts with Asia simply cannot be substantiated. The slave trade as a factor in the modern history of East Africa does not trace its roots back thousands of years (*p. 4*).[22]

Alpers continues his demolition work:

Further evidence that the slave trade was by no means prominent in East Africa before the eighteenth century comes from the Portuguese. Surely the Portuguese, as the pioneers of the Atlantic slave trade, would have tried to exploit the slave trade in East Africa had they found it to be already flourishing. But the early Portuguese chroniclers only mention the slave trade in passing. Much more important were the gold and ivory trades to Arabia and India. It is to these products that the Portuguese invaders turned their attention throughout the sixteenth and seventeenth centuries…. (*p. 5*).[23]

Returning to Reader, it is clear that in making his arguments for slavery in sub-Saharan Africa, he ignores some critical factors, in particular cultural factors, that would weaken his assessment of the plight of African farmers in historical times. His explanatory realities run up against other realities that do not stand in service of his point of view. And even when he mentions them, he does so in such a way to prevent them from disrupting the line of his reasoning. He mentions—but hardly in a comprehensive manner—African village communalism and the inclination of villagers to have large families. So, were the villages sparsely populated or densely populated? Which is it? "Society measured a man's standing by the number of children he had produced" he reveals. (*p. 253*).[24]/What Reader does not explain are the many legitimate reasons for the common practice of having large families: economic (providing unpaid labour for agriculture and husbandry, yet Reader talks about slaves being used for these activities); social/marital (to ensure survival of the community); even martial (strength in numbers, which could prove helpful in resolving tensions or hostilities with a troublesome neighbouring community).

UBUNTU: AN ANTI-SLAVERY STIMULUS

Within the confines of the discussion, Reader fails, glaringly, to mention *Ubuntu*, which is a significant philosophical aspect of the lifestyle of the African villager and an especially strong disincentive to the practice of slavery. *Ubuntu* leads away from any form of bondage.

Through its practice, as an idealistic way of living, villagers located and found themselves in each other, displaying humanity towards one another. Everywhere in sub-Saharan African village life we encounter corporate solidarity. Individual action had to consider communal corporate interests. The welfare and collective interests of the community would always take precedence over the rights and personal freedom of the individual or a handful of individuals. Over the centuries, *Ubuntu* has played a critical role in shaping the communal character of the village, by emphasizing human interconnectedness and group solidarity which builds up and sustains the esprit de corps of the village. An offshoot of this empathetic institution is cooperative economics and politics—people working together, helping one another; not oppressing and enslaving one another to accomplish common goals. In their book, *The Psychology of Blacks*, Afrocentric African American psychologists Joseph L. White and Adisa Ajamu, in discussing "the African worldview" make the following observations:

> The basic human unit is the tribe, not the individual. The tribe operates under a set of rules geared toward collective survival. Cooperation is therefore valued above competition and individualism. The concept of alienation is nonexistent in African philosophy since the people are closely interconnected with each other in a way of life that involves concern and

responsibility toward others. In a framework that values collective survival, where people are psychologically interdependent on each other, active aggression against another person is in reality an act of aggression against oneself (*1999, p. 12*).[25]

What those who choose to frame slavery in the manner mentioned earlier fail to realize or choose to ignore is that Africans were never engaged in an internal trafficking of enslaved individuals. They did not, as a rule, sell family members or their kinsmen for profit to African buyers in African markets to satisfy domestic labour needs before the intrusions of outsiders. Reader informs us "there is no evidence that market places or professional merchants were a feature of African village life in the sixth century AD. So long as barter remained the principal means of exchange in sub-Saharan African villages, trade did not stimulate the emergence of professional merchants. Individuals and groups exchanged produce and services directly among themselves, item for item: a week's labour for a share of the harvest; a goat for a hoe" (*pp. 267-268*).[26]

With Arab and European influences acting upon the lives of its members, however, strong villages were soon equipped and incentivized, generally speaking, to raid nearby vulnerable villages and sell people who looked like them but were in fact strangers to them. Also, Africans did not go in search of Arabs or Europeans to initiate and maintain either the trans-Saharan or trans-Atlantic slave "trade" (a misnomer if ever there was one, because there was nothing honorable or legitimate about this "trade" in terrified human flesh) nor did they organize the snaking caravans across the Sahara or own the ships or the plantations that accommodated the men and women doomed to a short lifetime of bondage on plantations in the Americas.

OBSESSIVE CLAIMS BEING MADE

As such, Africans did not create the trans-Atlantic market for human beings. Their pre-monetized village economies did not need foreign exchange for international trade; these were largely self-sufficient subsistence communities. And the African culprits co-opted into the "trade" certainly did not collaborate with Europeans to determine the practices, regulations and laws that would govern and eventually ruin the lives of the enslaved in the New World. They played absolutely no part in shaping the institution and its destructive impact on the lives of the enslaved in that part of the world. Furthermore, as explained by Stanley Elkins, Africans had no inkling about the terrible fate that awaited the unfortunates who became victims of the western system in the New World. In all probability, the complicit African chiefs, not wise to the ways of the western world which they never visited, must have assumed that the relationships of dependency with which they were familiar would be replicated in the New World. Elkins enlightens us:

> Slavery, of course, existed in Africa. But there was a sharp distinction between the domestic slavery prevalent among the tribes themselves and the state into which the deported captives would ultimately be delivered by the Europeans. There was little in the one that could prepare a man for what he would experience in the other. The typical West African slave was a recognized member of a household and possessed numerous rights. "A slave," according to R. S. Rattray, writing of Ashanti society, "might marry; own property; himself own a slave; swear an 'oath'; be a competent witness; and ultimately might become heir to his master *(Elkins, 1976, p. 96)*.[27]

Another historian, Gwendolyn Midlo Hall, acknowledges different sub-Saharan African labour systems, but she burdens them all, by insinuation, with the questionable label of "slavery," which leaves the reader with the misleading impression that almost all, if not all, workers in sub-Saharan Africa were enslaved, not unlike the conclusion we are led to by Elkins despite the many rights he recognized the so-called slave enjoyed in sub-Saharan Africa. In doing so, Hall trips herself up with that self-defeating declaration. She undermines her own position by insensitively using the loaded term "slavery" to categorize the different labour systems in sub-Saharan Africa. Basically, her contention is that every labour system in Africa constituted a form of slavery. As a result, she muddies the water of her exposition through a conflationary sleight of hand:

> There was a vast distinction between slavery in Africa and slavery in the Americas. Many forms of labor systems existed in sub-Saharan Africa. They involved a variety of mutual obligations. Many different words were used for the various forms of slavery. In Africa, slavery was often a system of incorporation into the society (*Hall, 2006, p. 11*).[28]

These observations raise a number of important questions. Given the distinct and vastly different nature of the two institutions (in the Americas and Africa), is it accurate to say, as Elkins does, that "Slavery, of course, existed in Africa"? Implicit in Elkins' assertion is the observance: "How could it be otherwise?" His claim has an air of inevitability and naturalness about it, as if Africans, due to their peculiar DNA, are genetically disposed to be born slaves, in the way Europeans understood that status and role, or as if it is in the nature of Africans to instinctively enslave one another for monetary gain in the way Europeans did it, despite the fact that African villagers, the main victims of westernized slavery, lived in remote pre-monetized subsistence economies when the Atlantic slave "trade" was initiated. Why then Elkins' use of the phrase "of course"? In using that phrase Elkins shows off a clear bias which predisposes him to find or to ascribe to sub-Saharan African culture(s) the practice of slavery, whether justifiable or not.

There seems to be an obsessive determination—as an European/American exculpatory tactic—to link Africans to slavery in every conceivable way. And Hall, as indicated, is not without guilt in this regard. But the more important question that must engage our attention is this. Did Africans originally designate or label their very different labour practices or labour systems "slavery" or was that word inserted into their languages and life experiences by Arab and European interlopers who willfully misrepresented and corrupted indigenous African forms of subordinate, dependent relationships? According to Hall, "Some scholars claim that before the Portuguese arrived, there was no word for 'slave' in the Bantu languages of West Central Africa" (*p. 12*).[29] Is that because slavery was not practised in sub-Saharan Africa? Yet Hall roots all systems of labour in sub-Saharan Africa in slavery. Conventional wisdom validates the assumption that slavery in Africa cannot and should not be contested because slavery in Africa is to be regarded as an almost organic social phenomenon. It seems the mere say-so of Western scholars (and now today's *Wikipedia*) is more than enough proof of that fact.

WESTERNIZING AFRICAN 'SLAVERY'

It can be argued nevertheless that African war captives became "slaves" only because of Arab and, more particularly, European social and economic need and greed. They were anything but, before that. An inflection point was reached when Europeans, and the Arabs before them, penetrated traditional African societies and facilitated the capture and acquisition of their residents for slavery. If there was a superabundance of slaves in these communities before they were penetrated, how were they used, what were they doing as slaves? And if they were kept as slaves, why were they sold to Arabs and Europeans in such large numbers as surplus labour, if they were serving a useful purpose in African states and village communities? Wouldn't that have occasioned great inconvenience because of the depletion of this significant source of much-needed labour (given the numbers involved) in those states and communities? Could it be that slaves were born and multiplied rapidly in number because a market (first Arab, then European), with an insatiable appetite for coerced labour, was created for them?

In one of his most recent works, *Challenging the Boundaries of Slavery (2003)*, David Brion Davis, examining the intimate hand-in-glove relationship between colonization and slavery dating back to the

Crusades and the pivotal role played by Venetian and Genoese merchants in fostering that bond, notes:

> Italian merchants had no scruples about selling thousands of Christian slaves to the Muslims of Egypt and Syria. At first they victimized the Slavic inhabitants of the Dalmatian coast, whose ethnic designation in Latin, sclavus=Slav, became the origin of the word for slave in English and other Western European languages: esclave in French; esclavo in Spanish; sklave in German. It's notable that the Hebrew, Greek, and Latin words for slave carried no ethnic connotations (ebed, doulos, servus). At first Slavic captives had been transported across Germany and France to Muslim Spain. But following the Western capture of Constantinople in 1204 in the Fourth Crusade, the Italians established slave "trading" posts along the northern coast of the Black Sea and the Sea of Azov, much as later European merchants would do along the western coast of Africa. The Genoese and Venetians purchased captive Armenians, Mingrelians, Russians and Tatars and Bulgarians – slaves who were no more a distinct people than the so-called Negroes who later ended up as New World slaves. The "Slav" slaves were highly prized in Egypt, Syria, Cyprus, Sicily, eastern Spain, and other Mediterranean markets. They were used for the production of sugar as well as for numerous other tasks (*pp. 17-18*).[30]

Another historian, Bernard Lewis, also informs us that "The Arabs practiced a form of slavery, similar to that which existed in other parts of the ancient world. The Qur'an accepts the institution, though it may be noted that the word *'abd* (slave) is rarely used, being more commonly replaced by some periphrasis such as *ma malakat aymanukum*, 'that which your right hands own'" *(Lewis, 1990, pp 5-6)*.[31] Venturing further into the discussion, Lewis adds:

> Already in medieval times [*in the Muslim world*] it became customary to use different words for black and white slaves. White slaves were normally called *mamluk*, an Arabic word meaning "owned," while black slaves were called *'abd*. In time, the word *'abd* ceased to be used of any but black slaves and eventually, in many Arabic dialects, simply came to mean a black man, whether slave or free. This transition from a social to an ethnic meaning is thus the reverse of the semantic development of our own word "slave," which began as the designation of an ethnic group and became a social term. In Western Islam—in North Africa and Spain—the word *khadim*, "servant" (dialectal form, *khadem*) is often specialized to mean "black slave," "slave woman," or "concubine." (*Lewis, 1990, p. 56*).[32]

If the term "slave," a designation first used to identify bonded whites, was little used by the Arabs, then how did this Slavic-derived term find its way into the mouths and everyday lives of African communities south of the Sahara? Arab slave owners who were familiar with Central and East European slaves generally tagged them *"Saqaliba"* (i.e., Slavs). The Slavs were a tribe of people inhabiting an area which now constitutes much of modern Poland. They suffered conquest by aggressive warlike Germanic tribes in 6 A.D. as a result of which they became a subject people, thereafter the term "Slav" and servitude became intimately connected.

The English term "slave" was first used in the 16th century. Prior to that, speakers of Medieval Latin (in use around A.D. 600 to about 1500) used the term *sclavus* and preceding the medieval period, Roman Latin presented the so-called known world with the term *salavus*; both Latin words referred to a Slav captive. Philip D. Curtin sheds a bit more light on the evolution of the term "slave." He explains: "The classical Latin for 'slave' was *servitus*, but slaves were so frequently Slavs from the east that *servitus* dropped out of Medieval Latin beginning in the ninth century and *sclavus* took its place, becoming the root of 'slave' in English and of cognates in Arabic and most European languages" (*Curtin in Mintz, 1974, p. 18*).[33]

So that the word "slave" obviously has no legitimate African etymology because the practice of servitude, so-called, in African societies, with its "rights-in-persons" principle operational, has been likened to the dynamics of an arranged marriage in motion, involving mutual dependence and obligations. It did not involve brutal dehumanization, nor was it hereditary as characterized by westernized slavery.

Very intriguing questions therefore sprout from that curiosity about the presence of the term "slave" in the vocabularies of traditional African communities. For instance, was there at the point of first contact any semantic congruity between the European word "slave" and any word or term in the African languages spoken by the individuals from the various ethnic communities or villages who were impacted by slavery, whether as captors or captives? Was there, as such, an African synonym that would have suffered no loss in translation or would have needed no addition to conveniently corrupt or complete its meaning to match the European definition or understanding of what it would have meant to be a slave in the Americas?

Can we find a linguistic equivalent in any of the African communities affected by westernized slavery which, from the very beginning, would have confirmed, conveyed, or suggested an exact coincidence in meaning, intention, experience and understanding between the two practices? Is there any evidence for such semantic ratification? Or are Westerners using a totally alien and self-serving frame of reference to distort an African reality? Is the term "slavery," with all of its deservedly distasteful connotations, really an imposition by external, and particularly western, sources on African systems of supplementary labour, each one of those systems being rooted in a sort of patron-client relationship?

These questions are relevant and legitimate because in traditional African society the practice, far from dehumanizing the person, seemed to function more like an adoption system that provided supplementary labour rather than as a system of brutal degradation and enslavement of the individual. Such "bonded" individuals did not exist outside of society but, as pointed out by Gwendolyn Midlo Hall and many others, formed an important and valuable part of its social and economic fabric, and remained human beings in their own right. Even Elkins concedes that point as well.

Consider, for instance, the relationship in *Things Fall Apart* [34]/between Chinua Achebe's Okonkwo and the boy, whom Okonkwo called Ikemefuna and who, because of tragedy, had come into Okonkwo's life from an entirely different village. The boy continued to live and serve at the pleasure of Okonkwo, who had "ownership" claims on his life. However, a warm guardian-and-ward relationship, one bordering on an actual father-son relationship, developed between them until further tragedy separated them for all time. At no point was the word "slave" used to describe the boy's status. Thus, using the Okonkwo-Ikemefuna model of interpersonal relationships as one of our guiding lights, we ask, is "slavery" a misleading misnomer that contaminates our view and understanding of those particular non-familial relationships that would have bound one individual to another in traditional sub-Saharan African village life?

AFRICAN SLAVERY'S ACCIDENTAL BIRTH

Did Europeans, originally ignorant and generally brimming with contempt for the cultural facts and ethos of African village life, see what they wanted to see and believe what they wanted to believe about African cultural practices and gave those phenomena whatever western labels suited their needs and prejudices? Was there, in other words, a malicious, willful, warped misunderstanding by Europeans of what they had witnessed?

An African proverb explains that "outsiders only see what they already know." In effect, human beings view the world and interpret what they witness through the eyes and mind of their specific cultures, their countries' historical experiences as well as their own private life experiences. Those are their inevitable reference points. Did Europeans therefore innocently or mischievously engage in cultural conversion and automatically or conveniently see a westernized master-slave relationship, where none actually existed, in order to further their own perverse economic ends?

Backed by formidable persuasive power, both cultural and military, Europeans were obviously able to force a reconceptualization, reframing and reinterpretation of those reciprocal social relationships they encountered and insinuate an unwholesome exploitative subordination into those relationships that linked weaker or less powerful individuals to stronger more dominant individuals. They misrepresented them in ways guaranteed to facilitate, justify and advance their (i.e., the Europeans') predatory economic agenda.

Among the Bambara of Mali, for instance, can be found the *woloso* caste. The *wolosos* (translated literally as, "ones born in the house") or house-captives were, according to Malian writer and social scientist, Amadou Hampate Ba, "servants or servant families attached for generations to one household [*i.e., to single households*]. Tradition allowed them … considerable material rights over their masters' possessions." (*Hampate Ba, 1979, p. 21*).[35] Also, among the Fulani of West Africa, orphaned children would be adopted by benevolent community members to whom they would owe, as a quid pro quo for saving their lives and rearing them, lifelong service, in the same way that biological kin are attached and committed to their sustaining family for life. Would non-acculturated colonizing Europeans, on encountering such people, have automatically labelled them "slaves" based on a misunderstanding of their deferential relationship to the families of the households to which they were attached in one way or another? Would the *wolosos* have been considered house-born slaves by Westerners?

THE 'MASTER-SLAVE' CURIOSITY

Those distinctive social relationships invite an interrogation of the contradictory concept (no doubt western in origin since the word "slave" did not originate with Africans) of the "slave-owning slave," an extraordinary entity, to say the least. Should the "slave" who owns a "slave" (or other "slaves") be socially stratified as a master or a slave or should he be categorized as a "master-slave"? The idea of a slave "owning" other slaves is, prima facie, an oxymoronic absurdity, a legal conundrum. It is totally unrealistic. The claim is made without any explicit etiological exposition about its genesis. John Reader offers an explanation about how this remarkable situation may have or would have emerged: "Some slaves with specialized skills acquired economic power in their own right; slaves with the appropriate aptitudes held important positions of trust and authority, and some even owned slaves of their own" (*1998, p. 295*).[36] In short, they had the means and so seized the opportunities to enjoy the prestige and power of being slave owners.

But, at a minimum, slave ownership connotes full selfhood on the part of the owner (or some degree of autonomy approximating that condition), personal power, independence, freedom of choice, action and defensible rights rooted in title and deed, which would mean that the slave-owning slave had some sort of legal personality and therefore should have been able to defend and emancipate himself judiciously using the law (as conceptualized by African villages) to attain that goal, unless he was fully comfortable in his enslavement. How would it have been possible for the slave to detach himself (legally, socially, and culturally) from the status of being a slave to become the owner/master of another human being as a slave? Would it have been possible to be a slave and not be a slave concurrently? How was it possible for "property" (the already owned slave) to exercise such judgement and right to independently acquire or own another human being as "property," resulting in property owning property?

What was the source of this peculiar power of the slave-owning slave? What recognized social and legal latitude allowed the "slave"—someone without power over his own person; someone whose freedom and rights were sharply curtailed or deemed non-existent; someone who was subject to the overriding authority and power of another—to assert this strange yet legitimate power to acquire another human being as a slave though he himself was a slave? Did he need his master's permission to become a slave-owner? What would happen if his master decided that he should not own another human being as a slave, could he, exercising an independent will and power, defy his master's expressed prohibition or would he have had to accede to his master's wish? Was there a limit on how many slaves a slave could own? It could only be that many (if not most or perhaps even all) of those in Africa south of the Sahara who were deemed "slaves" by Westerners were in fact not so. Walter Rodney, quoted earlier, says as much.

According to whose perspective and definition were such individuals considered or labelled "slaves"—by indigenous sources or foreign western sources? The available information strongly suggests they were deemed captives or social dependents, not slaves, by those who originally held them. They only became the slaves of Arabs and Westerners because of an opportunistic economic imagination—an everywhere-a-slave imagination. With that slaveholding mindset, opportunities for economic gain abounded in sub-Saharan Africa. Not only were there slaves aplenty on the continent but there were even, sui generis, slaves owning other slaves.

Reflecting further on this remarkable phenomenon of the slave-owning slave, we are forced to ask, if a slave owned other slaves, who commanded the latter: their direct owner (himself a slave) or the person who commanded their owner? In other words, how did authority flow in that situation? Given the slave-owning slave's status as a slave, did that status diminish or cause his authority over his slave(s) to be easily compromised and supplanted by the power of his master over his life? Could the slave's slave have appealed to his owner's master for redress in a situation of conflict or contention between himself and his subordinate slave-master? What would be the outcome of such disrespectful behaviour on the part of the slave's slave?

Could the master of the slave-owning slave, acting with impunity, inflict severe punishment on the latter's slave? Was the master answerable to his slave for any interactions he might have had with the latter's "human property" and how would having to adopt that subordinate position to his slave affect the master's authority over his slave-owning slave? Could his master have confiscated or killed the slave's slave, for instance, without compensating him for the loss? In other words, how secure or how powerful was the slave's ownership of other slaves? Is it also possible or conceivable that the master of the slave-owning slave might have been a "slave" himself, functioning only in the role of supervisor because of instructions coming from those above him?

In addressing this matter, one should not fail to contemplate the role of females. Bearing in mind that there were white slave mistresses, is it also possible that an enslaved female could have owned another female as a slave/handmaiden? If not, what would have prevented her from being able to do so? Gender, inferior social status, cultural constraints, religious restrictions, patriarchal prejudices, what? So, then, with the extensive blurring of these social and legal boundaries, who, in this context, is the master and who is the slave? What would have been the cut-off points of authority in those situations? Thus, it seems the fuzzy claim of the widespread westernized form of slavery being practised in Africa south of the Sahara must, at best, have resulted from the carte blanche misidentification of such individuals—meaning, a gross exaggeration, distortion and misreading of the facts; or, at worst, deliberate prevarication for economic gain, pure and simple.

MISUNDERSTANDING AFRICANITY

The problem of "slavery" in Africa south of the Sahara is linked to a European mindset and social experience filtering and (mis)interpreting/(mis)representing distinctive African realities to fit the mould of its own insight and understanding, thus converting the culturally unfamiliar into the culturally familiar with resulting distortions. Stated somewhat differently, the problem is rooted in poor cultural translations leading to misunderstandings and false narratives. The same would also have to be true for Arabs. Because of misinterpretation, were they guilty of corrupting our understanding of African social concepts, practices, and institutions? It seems then that not only did they change the perspective on these relationships by reframing them, but they conveniently, opportunistically, and deliberately mischaracterized their very nature, making them exploitable for economic gain.

In this regard the question has been asked: "Can two people see the same world in totally different ways, based on their personal frames of reference?" And the answer, according to the average social psychologist, is most assuredly yes; even identical twins, as discrete entities occupying separate bodies, experience the world differently. But would it be true to say that the mistaken identity of slaves made by Westerners was genuinely accidental or cunningly deliberate? Is it possible to give them the benefit of the doubt? Should one be so charitable?

On this matter of understanding, or rather misunderstanding, enslaved Africans and their ethnic social arrangements, historian Michael Craton has had this to say:

> Many plantocratic writers such as [Richard] Ligon, [Hans] Sloane, [Robert] Leslie, [Edward] Long, [William] Beckford and [Bryan] Edwards do provide sociological and anthropological information, as it were between the lines. Yet usually the language, besides the perception, is dangerously imprecise, if not

loaded. As Sidney Mintz has pointed out, what claim of superior understanding of 'primitive kinship,' for example, can properly be made by a people whose language uses the same word, 'brother-in-law,' for wife's brother and sister's husband, thus failing to distinguish two diametrically different kinship links? (*Craton, 1974, p. 45*).[37]

The extent and nature of the problem of western incomprehension of African culture(s) and social realities is made quite clear by English-Kenyan writer Beryl Markham who states in her 1942 memoir *West with the Night*, "Africa is mystic; it is wild…It is what you will and it withstands all interpretations." Africa, as a result, was considered the ultimate Other because its peoples, with their special qualities and distinctions, before becoming westernized, presented a puzzling contrast with the rest of humanity. There were obvious differences in physical traits, such as facial features, colour of skin and type of hair, accentuated by sharp cultural differences which were evident by their general deportment, the languages they spoke, the way they dressed and the values they prized. Which is a point made abundantly clear by British historian Basil Davidson:

> For many centuries Africa and its people seemed mysterious and even perverse to the rest of the world…. Where had Africans come from? Why were they so different from other men? What was the

explanation for their strange customs, so unlike those of Europe?

Many answers were proposed, but most of them served only to deepen the darkness that surrounded the image of Africa. At last the Europeans resorted to an easy conclusion—one that reflected their inability to judge any culture except in terms of their own. Africans, they decided, were just savages, inferior beings, and had always been so (*Davidson, 1966, p.17*).[38]

More recently, anthropologist Ivan Karp points out:

Africa has been perceived by some Westerners as a continent of peoples whose customs and manners are incomprehensible.... A further complication arises because the languages, social organization, history, and environments of Africa are so different from our own. These differences are intensified by prevailing attitudes about other cultures. Westerners tend to think that technological achievements have given them command and control of the world and that all other societies should emulate them (*Karp, 1986, p. 199*).[39]

J. H. Kwabena Nketia has provided us with a practical illustration of this incomprehension. The Ghanaian ethnomusicologist, composer and writer explains that the Ashanti were well aware that their social customs were not easily or ever really understood by Westerners, especially British colonial officials, and they coined an expression that reflected that awareness. He writes:

"There is an Ashanti expression used when someone hears something but does not appear to understand it, or when he looks somewhat unconvinced. It says, 'It is like singing to the White man.' The person hears what goes on and seems to give it polite attention, but he is not moved because he really does not understand it" (*Nketia in Mintz, 1974, p. 153*).[40]

Such is the conceit of man that when he is ignorant in a situation where he is expected to be knowledgeable, he often feigns wisdom by mentally cobbling together an ill-fitting picture of what the truth or reality before him represents. In other words, the reality is subjectively revised to fit the mould of his consciousness and the extent of his knowledge in order to bring the phenomenon or situation under his control. Prejudice would have told the British the social customs were nothing more than crude simplicities forged by lesser beings or primitives. These were not matters that demanded close attention and evaluation. Business writer and investor Morgan Housel, author of *The Psychology of Money (2020)*, explains the process this way:

> Most people, when confronted with something they don't understand, do not realize they don't understand it because they are able to come up with an explanation that makes sense based on their own unique perspective and experiences in the world, however limited those experiences are. We all want the

complicated world we live in to make sense. So we tell ourselves stories to fill in the gaps of what are effectively blind spots [*or information deficits in our understanding of the world*] (*p. 199*).[41]

To complete the illustration, Nketia explains the Ashanti would play a song as an anti-colonial protest for the representative of the British crown whenever he had official meetings with their chiefs. This was their convention for all of the colonial period. The song was composed to warn of their intended conquest of their most difficult foe, the Adinkra. Its translated title read: "Slowly but surely we shall kill Adinkra." The beaming Briton, unknowingly acting as surrogate for the Adinkra, went about greeting the chief or chiefs undisturbed by the music, not recognizing the hostile intent of their "greeting." Nketia comments, "Like the earlier travelers and administrators who wrote about African music, he would hear the piece without understanding it" (*Ibid*).[42] To be sure, western hubris would have assigned no particular significance to the song (even if understood) nor would it have ascribed such deadly cunning to Africans whom it would have regarded with unveiled contempt as dullards. For our benefit, Nketia expands our understanding by revealing that:

> Apart from the initial problem of "tuning in" to unfamiliar sound materials, to relate to African music,

one must appreciate not only its forms, structure, and modes of expression, but also any pragmatic or extramusical meaning embodied in it or associated with it by tradition. Since the symbols of extramusical meanings are not universal but culturally defined, what a piece conveys beyond its sensuous or surface structure can only be grasped by those acquainted with its background (*p. 159*).[43]

CONTEMPT FOR THINGS AFRICAN

Indifferent to such cognitions, the colonial attitude towards Africans was dismissive: they lacked history and their cultures were coarse. That attitude buttressed by their toxic mindset justified and made it easy for the Ashanti to reciprocate the contempt of the British by ridiculing the governor. Indeed, the historical habit of western civilization has been to present dominant images of the world that favour its own cultural identity and greatness while often diminishing others, especially Africans, through devastating prejudice and mixed messages. As far as they are concerned, the western oyster is the only real world containing reliable valuable knowledge.

This attitude has made them (certainly as colonialists of the past and white supremacists of the present) intolerant of other people's points of view as well as doctrinaire and highly opinionated. And in their opinion, their view is invariably the right view. But Karp's advice is that "the beginning of a dialogue involves trying to think the thoughts other people think, and in their own language." (*Karp, 1986, p. 200*).[44] That advice went largely unheeded by the vast majority of colonialists who considered African languages unrefined gibberish at best, primate chatter at worst, not deserving of respectful attention and not to be used routinely, and therefore not to be learned, as mediums of intelligent communication. Such languages, irritating or amusing to the colonial ear, would contaminate the tongue and the mind.

One can only conclude then that the term "slave" is a distorting externally imposed code word attached to distinctive African social relationships. That subversive word would have gained social meaning, significance, and acceptance over time by impacted traditional African communities, even though it obviously did not originate with them. Whether authentically formulated, inherited, or bequeathed, words in themselves have no inherent meaning; they are basically arbitrary symbols. But they are given meaning by culture-bound human beings who, through consensus, decide and accept that those words should signify or represent specific things or notions.

LINGUISTIC MISUNDERSTANDINGS

As an expression of culture, language is a living thing, often incorporating neologisms, foreign terms, concepts, and definitions considered useful and relevant into daily practice and speech while discarding old words and ideas that have lost their usefulness or relevance for the evolving society. That appropriation is not without consequences because, as explained by J. Ki-Zerbo, "Every language is both a psychological entity and a social phenomenon. Its vocabulary, for instance, reflects the impact of history on a people. But conversely it is the language, the 'word', that instills a system of concepts and behavioural rules into a people's mentality and motivations" (*Ki-Zerbo, 1981; 2000, p. 352*).[45]

Adoption of a foreign language, or significant parts thereof, is, insidiously, a conduit for cultural penetration, psychological influence, and control. It is more than just learning and using different words for familiar things. Language possesses the power to call reality into existence because it describes and names things. In other words, it gives rise to, shapes and places limits on human consciousness and understanding of the immaterial and material world surrounding the individual. It tells the individual what exists, what is real, and how to think about internal and external reality. Thus, it can change insight and understanding through structuring and restructuring perceptions and thought processes. It is learning another nuanced way to see, define, evaluate, think critically, and conceptualize about familiar and unfamiliar things. It can constrict, expand, or distort the boundaries of socio-cognitive reality. As pointed out by

Charles Bird and Martha Kendall, "Language in all of its forms reverberates against a background of cultural understanding and assumptions without which it remains vague and imprecise" (*Bird & Kendall, 1987, p. 14*).[46]

Briefly stated, different languages determine different cosmo-visions and worldviews. Thus, (and this is not only true for an Orwellian *1984* dystopia of doublespeak), whoever controls the language controls its concepts and definitions; whoever controls the concepts and definitions controls thought processes and reasoning; whoever controls thought processes and reasoning controls insight and understanding of the world; and whoever controls insight and understanding of the world will pre-determine the outcome (i.e. the conclusions) of any analytical discourse about the world. They can impose their worldview on others. That may be the explanation here for African villages being accused by (mistranslating or ignorant or deliberately deceptive) Westerners of practising westernized "slavery."

Given those realities, it becomes clear that African historians themselves have been co-opted by their Western mentors and interlocutors into adopting western terminology and a western cultural perspective and frame of reference to rename, describe and analyze their own realities as to whether pre-colonial sub-Saharan Africa had a superabundance of slaves. Reader mentions one history of slavery in Africa which claims that "between 30 to 60 per cent of the entire population were slaves during historical times" (*1998, p. 291*).[47] African scholars do not challenge these claims because, it seems, their independence as scholars has been usurped by their Western mentors/academic supervisors.

DELEGITIMIZING AFRICAN PERSPECTIVES

A case in point being the experience of Senegalese historian, anthropologist, and physicist Cheikh Anta Diop who was forced to present three different doctoral theses to get his PhD (History), because his thinking and scholarly insights—about the cultural unity of the African continent, with ancient Egypt as its foundation, and with his identification of ancient Egyptians as black people— did not line up with ethnocentric western thinking and insights: that is, Egypt, which has always been an inextricable geographic part of Africa, long before Arabs invaded and staked their claim to the country, with its immensely impressive technological accomplishments, was to be considered the southern extension of Europe. Westerners have always felt entitled to police the work of African scholars and determine what is valid and acceptable and what is not. Thus, it is no surprise that, with imperialist penetration and colonial occupation, the socio-obstetrical "fact" of sub-Saharan African slavery has become entrenched in the mind of the world. Even so, it is highly unlikely that the millions of captured Africans who made the forced journey across the Atlantic to the New World self-identified as slaves.

Consequently, we are compelled to ask how precise, how useful, can the assertion be that European countries shipped "12 million African slaves" (not counting the Atlantic's watery trail of death) to the New World? Did the victims whose lives were violently disrupted by raiders actually think of and identify themselves as slaves, participants in punitive or voluntary servitude, or were they just ordinary free villagers, taken unawares, suddenly deprived of their freedom, and then thrown helter skelter into a disastrous situation not of their making, yet labelled "slaves," thus undermining the claim of widespread slavery in sub-Saharan Africa? Were they designated and living as slaves prior to and at the point of their capture and did they themselves acknowledge and accept the status of slaves? If they did not, how then can it even be thought, suggested, claimed, or admitted that they were slaves? Consider the attitude and behaviour of Alex Haley's Kunta Kinte, the free African, in Roots who resisted being identified as a slave before being forced violently to accept his fate as Toby, the New World slave. His coercive transformation, which required the spilling of his blood and severe mutilation, is reflective of the experience of many labelled "slaves" who did not self-identify that way.

Thus, it is difficult to imagine that we can be led along the right path by European historians, invested in the glory of colonial conquest and rule and convinced of their own superiority and the natural subservience of Africans, to make proper accurate objective assessments of bondage and colonialism in sub-Saharan Africa. Until Africans took control of their historical narrative, the world was starved of accounts which were accommodative of African initiative and their reaction to slavery and colonialism. Philip D. Curtin observes: "In colonial Africa … the Europeans who left the records had rarely grown up in the society they observed; they rarely understood its language or culture, and were unsympathetic with the parts they did understand. Thus their record is inadequate in the extreme" (*Curtin in Mintz, 1974, pp. 17-18*).[48/]

It is clear that in arriving at a precise understanding of "bondage" in sub-Saharan Africa, many linguistic, cultural, and philosophical hurdles will have to be jumped. The fact is even highly traditional societies, far from being "static," do change. They do not stand perfectly still with the passage of time. In the quest to discover whether the term "slave" has any authentic African roots or whether some other term was used by Africans to describe the status of an obligated subordinate in relation to a commanding superior, the pilgrimage to the truth could be misdirected because of deliberate distortion and gross misrepresentation. Linguist Walter J. Ong fortifies this perspective by explaining that "You cannot without serious and disabling distortion describe a primary phenomenon by starting with a subsequent secondary phenomenon and paring away the differences. Indeed, starting backwards in this way—putting the car[t] before the horse—you can never become aware of the real differences" *(Ong, 1982; 2002, p. 13).*[49]

Very likely the term "slave" must have displaced the original pre-colonial term(s) used by African oral communities to label the obligated worker and since the spoken word, unlike the written or printed, is highly perishable, because it disappears at the point of actual speech and only survives into the future, if at all, through memory and repetition, the mystery surrounding the power to name and accurately define the institution of "slavery" and its victims in a sub-Saharan African context may never be solved. Which does not mean that failure should be the expected outcome of such research and, as such, absolutely no effort should be made towards discovery. What it does mean is that the real original term(s) used by those oral communities, which would help to clarify the social significance of such relationships, may or may not be lost forever. As explained in *The UNESCO Courier (May 1977, p. 8),*[50] "the meanings of words [*in oral societies*] are understood by reference to practical situations which members of the group have experienced." Indirectly, this explanation refers to the distorting cultural impact and lasting effect well-placed, truly powerful, influential, extraneous sources can have on the way social reality is perceived, interpreted, and defined in oral societies.

With the displacement of the original African term(s), the indigenous institution very likely suffered reinterpretation and recasting in a light very different from the original indigenous source of its illumination by those who, brimming with contempt and antipathy for the peoples and their cultures, lacked an insider's knowledge of the communities they attacked and subjected to their reckless predations. They lacked the basic respect, direct experience, necessary revelation, and linguistic expertise to make an easy go of transliteration or accurate interpretation of what they had encountered. Moreover, as already pointed out, their languages may have lacked suitable corresponding words and terms to capture the essence of what they saw and heard from the indigenes. And while it is true that there is nothing like local knowledge, thus tempting the enquirer to turn to the oral historians of those communities, namely, their griots, in the hope of discovering the truth, such interaction may not yield much fruit in the way of enlightenment. Commenting on the powerful impact of the present and its current pressing social needs in re-shaping the past of oral society, Ong has offered these words of caution:

> Oral societies can be characterized as homeostatic. That is to say, oral societies live very much in the present which keeps itself in equilibrium or homeostasis by sloughing off memories which no longer have present relevance....
>
> Oral cultures of course have no dictionaries and few semantic discrepancies. The meaning of each word is controlled by ... 'direct semantic ratification', that is by the real-life situations in which the word is used here and now. The oral mind is uninterested in definitions....

Memory of the old meaning of old terms thus has some durability, but not unlimited durability.

> When generations pass and the object or institution referred to by the archaic word is no longer part of the present, lived experience, though the word has been retained, its meaning is commonly altered or simply vanishes.
>
> The present impose[s] its own economy on past remembrances.... oral traditions reflect a society's present cultural values rather than idle curiosity about the past (*Ong, 1982; 2002, pp. 46-48*).[51]

Ong's conclusion resonates sympathetically with the following observation made by Luther Lee Bernard, sociologist, social psychologist, and historian, in his book, *Introduction to Social Psychology (1926, p. 289)*. Concerning the preservation of meaning through "continuity in transmission" from one individual/group to another individual/group of the same socio-cultural character or background, Bernard states:

> The meaning of art and of science is not the function of the symbols which represent or condition them to us, but it resides in the persons whose responses, overt and internal or attitudinal, are conditioned to the symbols. The symbols are merely the communicative media which carry the meaning from one person to another through the process of conditioning by association. Once the chain of conditioned responses is broken by omitting a generation of men thus conditioned to respond psychically and overtly to these symbols, their meaning is gone. Such has actually happened at times in history, where whole systems of symbols, like the languages and the writing and culture of the Hittites and the Philistines and the Minoans have been lost because the chain of conditioned responses which preserved the meaning of their writings was broken. As yet no one has been able to recondition his responses to these symbols in the same way in which these ancient peoples had conditioned theirs and thus to interpret their meaning. Consequently their cultures are to us sealed books and their symbols have lost completely their original power of suggestion.[52]

SLAVERY UNKNOWN TO AFRICANS

What is manifestly clear, even at this point, is the undeniable fact that the African notion and practice of "slavery" involving human beings with restricted rights but who remained socially mobile and were integrated into the oral communities and households that received them, clearly did not coincide with the corrupt European/westernized notion and practice of slavery. Europeans reduced human beings to sub-human property, that is, chattel, without rights, and subjected them to constant brutalization and exclusion from every avenue of activity that would permit them to improve their lives, become socially mobile and be fully integrated as equals and respectable members into the many makeshift New World societies in which they found themselves. Moreover, "servitude" or "slavery" in African communities (if, indeed, the term ever enjoyed independent pre-colonial validity among Africans, given the absence of any institution even vaguely resembling westernized slavery in their communities), did not involve the automatic transfer of the status from parent to child. The individual, and not his progeny, was "enslaved" or "bonded." The descendants of those bonded were never robbed of their humanity and were in fact automatically granted their freedom and became integrated as legitimate members of the host society. Even the so-called slaves in sub-Saharan Africa were incorporated into the societies where they resided.

Thus, it seems westernized slavery in sub-Saharan Africa is rooted more in economic fantasy than in objective cultural, anthropological, and historical fact. That fantasy justified the so-called "trade" in African lives. Whatever existed and was practised in ancient sub-Saharan Africa, prior to the advent of Arabs and Europeans, as "bondage" should therefore not be identified in any way with westernized slavery. Perhaps, it should not even be called slavery, even with the best academic conjuring. Until trustworthy irrefutable evidence is provided to confirm the existence of slavery in ancient sub-Saharan Africa, we should curb our zeal to paint pre-colonial Africa with the slavery brush. We should in fact be extremely sceptical, cautious, and hesitant about accepting and using the term "slavery" loosely with reference to pre-colonial systems of labour on the continent.

About Trevor M. Millett: *He is a Graduate of the University of the West Indies (MA, History); author of The Chinese in Trinidad (1993); and a short story writer. He is an experienced print journalist who has worked in the Press Section (English) of the United Nations Department of Public Information (UN/DPI).*

REFERENCES

1. Thomas C. Foster: How to Write Like a Writer. (Harper/Perennial: New York, 2022), p. 233.

2. G. Mokhtar: Introduction in <u>UNESCO General History of Africa II: Ancient civilizations of Africa ed. G Mokhtar</u>, (California: UNESCO/Heinemann/Univ of California Press, 1981; 2000), p. 2.

3. Herodotus: The Histories. (London: Penguin Classics, 1996).

4. Amos N. Wilson: The Psychology of Self-Hatred and Self-Defeat: Towards a Reclamation of the Afrikan Mind. (New York: Afrikan World InfoSystems, 2019), pp. 101-102.

5. Chancellor Williams: The Rebirth of African Civilization. (Chicago: Third World Press, 2004), p. 69.

6. Ibid., p. 107.

7. Paul E. Lovejoy: Africa and Slavery (taken from Transformations in Slavery: A History of Slavery in Africa. Cambridge University Press: 1983) https://www.cambridge.org/core/books/history-of-sub-saharan-africa/slavery-in-

africa/3D60C8CO75A3BFACC9870DADD5A5
B3C5

8. John Reader: AFRICA: A Biography of the
Continent. (New York: Alfred A. Knopf, 1998),
pp. 252-253.

9. Ibid., p. 254.

10. Ibid., pp. 258-259.

11. Ibid., p. 289.

12. Ibid., p. 291.

13. Ibid., p. 249.

14. Ibid., p. 291.

15. Ibid., p. 367.

16. Walter Rodney: West Africa and the Slave-Trade.
Historical Association of Tanzania Paper No. 2
(Nairobi: East African Publishing House, 1967;
1970), p. 18.

17. Ibid., p. 17.

18. Edward A. Alpers: The East African Slave Trade.
Historical Association of Tanzania Paper No. 3
(Nairobi: East African Publishing House, 1967;
1974), p. 3.

19. Ibid.

20. Alpers., p. 4.

21. Ibid.

22. Ibid.

23. Alpers., p. 5

24. Reader: p. 253.

25. Joseph L. White & Adisa Ajamu: The Psychology of Blacks. (New Jersey: Prentice Hall, 1999), p. 12.

26. Reader: pp. 267-268.

27. Stanley M. Elkins: Slavery: A Problem in American Institutional and Intellectual Life. (Chicago: University of Chicago Press, 1959; 1976), p. 96.

28. Gwendolyn Midlo Hall: Slavery and African Ethnicities in the Americas: Restoring the Link. (Kingston (Jamaica)/Miami (Florida): Ian Randle Publishers, 2006), p. 11.

29. Ibid., p.12.

30. David Brion Davis: Challenging the Boundaries of Slavery. (Cambridge, Massachusetts: Harvard University Press, 2003), pp. 17-18.

31. Bernard Lewis: Race and Slavery in the Middle East. (New York: Oxford University Press, 1990), pp 5-6.

32. Ibid., p. 56.

33. Philip D. Curtin: The Black Experience of Colonialism and Imperialism in <u>Slavery, Colonialism and Racism ed. Sidney W. Mintz</u>, (New York: W.W. Norton & Co. Inc., 1974), p. 18.

34. Chinua Achebe: Things Fall Apart (AWS). London: Heinemann, 1969.

35. Amadou Hampate Ba: Tongues that span the centuries The faithful guardians of Africa's oral tradition in <u>The UNESCO Courier – Africa and its history A continent viewed from within, August-September 1979</u>. (Paris: UNESCO, 1979), p. 21.

36. Reader: p. 295.

37. Michael Craton: Searching for the Invisible Man Some of the Problems of Writing on Slave Society in the British West Indies in <u>Historical Reflections/Reflexions Historiques Volume 1, No. 1.</u> (Waterloo, Ontario: Dept. of History, University of Waterloo, 1974), p. 45.

38. Basil Davidson: Great Ages of Man: African Kingdoms. (New York: Time-Life Books, 1966), p. 17.

39. Ivan Karp: African Systems of Thought in <u>Africa ed. Phyllis M. Martin and Patrick O'Meara</u>. (Bloomington: Indiana University Press, 1986), p. 199.

40. J.H. Kwabena Nketia: The Musical Heritage of Africa in <u>Slavery, Colonialism and Racism ed. Sidney W. Mintz</u>, (New York: W.W. Norton & Co. Inc., 1974), p. 153.

41. Morgan Housel: The Psychology of Money: Timeless lessons on wealth, greed and happiness. (Hampshire: Harriman House Ltd, 2020), p. 199.

42. Nketia: p. 153.

43. Ibid., p. 159.

44. Karp: p. 200.

45. J. Ki-Zerbo: The interdisciplinary methods adopted in this study in <u>UNESCO General History of Africa I: Methodology and African Prehistory ed. J. Ki-Zerbo</u> (California: UNESCO/Heinemann/Univ of California Press, 1981; 2000), p. 352.

46. Charles S. Bird & Martha B. Kendall: The Mande Hero Text and Context in <u>Explorations in African Systems of Thought, ed. Ivan Karp &</u>

Charles S. Bird. (Smithsonian Institution Press: Washington, D.C. 1980; 1987), p. 14.

47. Reader: p. 291.

48. Curtin: pp. 17-18.

49. Walter J. Ong: Orality and Literacy. (London/New York: Routledge, 1982/2002), p. 13.

50. UNESCO: Africa rediscovers its cultural roots (Conclusions of the Intergovernmental Conference on Cultural Policies in Africa held in Accra, Ghana, 27 Oct.- 6 Nov. 1975) in The UNESCO Courier – The changing face of Africa, May 1977. (Paris: UNESCO, 1977), p. 8.

51. Ong: pp. 46-48.

52. Luther Lee Bernard: An Introduction to Social Psychology. (New York: Henry Holt and Co. 1926), p. 289.

ADDITIONAL READING

Chinweizu: Decolonising the African Mind. (Lagos, Nigeria: Pero Press, 1987)

David Brion Davis: Slavery and the Post-World War II Historians in Slavery, Colonialism and Racism ed. Sidney W. Mintz, (New York: W.W. Norton & Co. Inc., 1974), pp. 1-16

W.E. Burghardt Du Bois: The World and Africa: An inquiry into the part which Africa played in world history. (New York: International Publishers, 1946/1981).

Allan G.B. Fisher & Humphrey J. Fisher: Slavery and Muslim Society in Africa. (New York: Anchor Books, 1971).

J.O. Hunwick: Black Africans in the Islamic World: An Understudied Dimension of the Black Diaspora in The African Diaspora Tarikh 20 Vol. 5, No. 4., ed. A.I. Asiwaju & Michael Crowder, New Jersey: Longman, 1978, pp. 20-40.

J.E. Inikori: The Origin of the Diaspora: The Slave Trade from Africa in The African Diaspora

Tarikh 20 Vol. 5, No. 4., ed. A.I. Asiwaju & Michael Crowder, (New Jersey: Longman, 1978), pp. 1-20.

A.L. Mabogunje: Historical geography: economic aspects in UNESCO General History of Africa I: Methodology and African Prehistory ed. J. Ki-Zerbo. (California: University of California Press, 1983; 2000), pp. 333-347.

Chancellor Williams: The Destruction of Black Civilization: Great Issues of a Race From 4500 B.C. To 2000 A.D. (Chicago: Third World Press, 1992).

Made in the USA
Middletown, DE
12 May 2023